Parents' Quick Start Recovery Guide:

Finding Help Fast When Your Child or Teen Has an Eating Disorder

Lori Osachy, MSS, LCSW

Lori Osachy provides counseling and parent coaching for anorexia, bulimia, compulsive eating and related mental health issues at her clinic in Jacksonville, Florida. For information on parent consults, call 904-737-3232. Lori is a licensed clinical social worker (LCSW) and holds a Master of Social Service (MSS). Following are expressions of gratitude from former clients and their parents.

e-mail: bodyimagecounseling@gmail.com.
Visit her website at www.bodyimagecounseling.com

"It is somewhat painful to recount my state, when I was in the depths of my eating disorder and first began treatment with Lori. I had tried for some time to recover on my own. Lori helped me realize how I was using my eating disorder as a coping mechanism. **Lori may have saved my life.** *Lori helped me rebuild my life."* - Sarah, age 23

"I want to thank you for all that you've done for me and all that you've helped me to accomplish over this past year. Your compassion, positiveness and endless patience, as well as your kind and gentle nature, provided me with clarity, insight, encouragement, hope for a better future, and comfort when I wasn't able to find it elsewhere. You are inspiring and I am so grateful to have met you. ***Thank you for your patience and understanding and for being a friend to me when I felt like I had no one."***
- Karli, age 20

"I have struggled with bulimia for almost two years! **I have gone to many therapists and Lori has definitely been the most help!** *Lori has given me the confidence that this will not take over my life and I am now much happier."*
- **Amanda, age 19**

"At the age of 15, my beautiful daughter was in the depths of anorexia. Watching my daughter self- destruct was scary. Not being able to help... frightening. The extreme weight loss, excessive exercise, panic attacks, and worse... Lori was able to gain my daughter's trust and gave us the tools, sound advice, and confidence to control her (our) life. **Thank you for being the 'life line' that pulled my daughter away from the edge.***"*
- **A proud and grateful father**

"My sessions at The Body Image Counseling Center have helped me rebuild the foundation of my being. I have learned so much about myself and have been given tools which have improved who I am today. **I would like to thank Lori with all my heart for helping me overcome a lifelong struggle with food** *with her support, patience and kindness."* - **Jenny, age 39**

"THANK YOU so much for all your help - I seriously have no idea what I would have done without you. I never thought that I would be able to reach this place in recovery - **I honestly think that I'm on the road to a COMPLETE recovery this time** *and I definitely have you to thank!"*
- **Lauren, age 28**

Parents' Quick Start Recovery Guide: Finding Help Fast When Your Child or Teen Has an Eating Disorder.

All contents copyright © 2012 by Lori Osachy, MSS, LCSW.
All rights reserved.

ISBN-13:978-1479205004
ISBN-10:1479205001

No part of this document or the related files may be reproduced or transmitted in any form, by any means (electronic, photocopying, recording, or otherwise) without the prior written permission of the author or publisher.

Limit of Liability and Disclaimer of Warranty: The publisher has used her best efforts in preparing this book, and the information provided herein is provided "as is." Lori Osachy, MSS, LCSW makes no representation or warranties with respect to the accuracy or completeness of the contents of this book and specifically disclaims any implied warranties of merchantability or fitness for any particular purpose and shall in no event be liable for any loss, including but not limited to special, incidental, consequential, or other damages. The advice in this book is based on generally accepted workable principles, but, as every human being is unique, said principles may not be applicable to your particular situation. Therefore, the publisher and author assume no responsibility for damages based on the reader's reliance on any advice, principles, or information contained herein.

Trademarks: This book identifies product names and services known to be trademarks, registered trademarks, or service marks of their respective holders. They are used throughout this book in an editorial fashion only. In addition, terms suspected of being trademarks, registered trademarks, or service marks have been appropriately capitalized, although Lori Osachy, MSS, LCSW cannot attest to the accuracy of this information. Use of a term in this book should not be regarded as affecting the validity of any trademark, registered trademark, or service mark. Lori Osachy, MSS, LCSW is not associated with any product or vendor mentioned in this book.

Dedication

*To the parents of children and teens with eating disorders–
Never give up – your child can live free from the pain of
eating disorders.*

Acknowledgements

Edited by Jordan Catapano
Designed by Jean Boles

Parents' Quick Start Recovery Guide:

Finding Help Fast When Your Child or Teen Has an Eating Disorder

Lori Osachy, MSS, LCSW

Table of Contents

Introduction: page 11
How this book can help your child get better fast

Chapter One: page 17
What happened to my child?

Chapter Two: page 23
How do I know for sure my child has an eating disorder?

Chapter Three: page 35
Five steps to setting up the best professional treatment team

1) Why your child developed an eating disorder, and what you can do to help her
2) Why you need to take her to the doctor FIRST
3) How to find a QUALIFIED eating disorder therapist
4) How to find a QUALIFIED dietitian
5) How to find a QUALIFIED psychiatrist

Chapter Four: page 75
Parent FAQs

1) We feel uncomfortable questioning doctors about their qualifications and background. Isn't this inappropriate and disrespectful to them?

2) What if our insurance does not cover any of the qualified and recommended therapists?

3) What if there are no qualified eating disorder treatment professionals in my area?

4) When is hospitalization necessary?

5) What if my child refuses to go for counseling?

6) What if my child is over 18 years old and refuses treatment, even though we know she is in trouble?

7) My child is an athlete. Are there any special considerations I should keep in mind?

8) How do I help my child feel better about her body image and weight when she lives in a society obsessed with dieting?

9) How are eating disorders different for boys, and how can we help our son recover quickly?

Chapter Five: page 95
Bonus Section:

The Seven Must-Read Tips for Building Healthy Body Self-Esteem in Children

About the Author: 101

INTRODUCTION

If you have bought this book, know that you are a wonderful parent. Even though you may be frightened, confused and frustrated by your child's eating disorder, you have summoned a great deal of courage to seek help rather than deny or minimize the problem.

This book is a guide for parents who have either just discovered that their child has an eating disorder and are overwhelmed with knowing the right steps to take, or who have known for a while but have been frustrated and dismayed in their attempts to find help that works. This guide will help you to quickly secure effective treatment for your son or daughter, and will likely save them from years of suffering from the devastating effects of anorexia, bulimia, and/or compulsive overeating. Additionally, in most cases your child can receive this help without having to enter an expensive inpatient eating disorder treatment program or spend years in costly counseling sessions.

Why should you listen to me? Because I am a licensed clinical social worker with over twenty years of experience working with children and young adults with eating disorders. I have worked in inpatient and outpatient eating disorder treatment settings and know what works and what doesn't. My patients have a high recovery rate: most of my clients show significant improvement within three to six months of treatment, and most achieve full recovery from their eating disorder symptoms. I do not ostracize parents of these children by blaming them for their child's disorder; rather, I include them as an integral part of their child's treatment team, acting as a coach to help them get their child better fast.

Over the years many people have asked me if it's depressing and draining to work with people who have eating disorders and their families. I honestly tell them that the opposite is true. I have been doing this work for so many years because I have the immense pleasure of watching children and teenagers get better. It is the most rewarding job in the world when you can help to restore peace and healing to young people and their families on a regular basis. An added plus is that most young people with eating disorders, AND their parents, are high achieving, sensitive, responsible, and motivated to get better; they just need the right person to guide them. It is truly a joy to work with them!

What I find very distressing, however, are the hundreds of parents who have called me over the years, desperate to find help that works for their child but cannot afford treatment, or, are confused and overwhelmed by the oftentimes conflicting advice they have received from the Internet, other treatment providers who are not qualified to treat eating disorders, or from well-meaning, but misguided family members. It is for these parents and their children that I wrote this guide. I try to at least have a conversation with every parent who calls me for help, even if they cannot afford treatment. I feel it is my responsibility as a therapist with expertise and success in treating eating disorders to share my knowledge with as many people as possible, and at the very least point them in the right direction towards help. By creating this guide, I am able to consolidate my knowledge in one place and make it accessible to many more people than I could by just answering phone calls and e-mails. Be reassured that this is the very same advice I would give if you came in to see me personally about your child's eating disorder.

This coaching course will cover the five essential steps that you can and must take immediately in order to help your child get on the road to permanent recovery. It provides concrete tools that you can start using today to help your child, including checklists for interviewing potential members of your child's outpatient treatment team, warning signs about when to keep looking, and techniques you should use at home to accelerate your child's recovery. There is an informative question and answer section featuring questions asked by real parents of children with eating disorders. Finally, there is a Must-Read section on how to help your other children avoid falling prey to an eating disorder.

I adore working with children, and especially with teenagers. For me it is a privilege and an honor when a young person trusts me enough to share their worries, insecurities, hopes, dreams, and struggles, and then allows me to serve as a trusted support and guide.

I am also a strong advocate and cheerleader for parents, especially since I am one myself! Parenting is a tumultuous and exciting journey, and as I'm sure you've realized, children don't come with a manual. The last thing parents need when their child is suffering with a life-threatening mental illness is to be told it's their fault, to be shut out of the treatment process, or to have their expertise about their own children discounted by the professionals involved in their child's care. Unfortunately, these situations can be all too common in the world of eating disorders treatment.

Many years ago, when I was first beginning my training as an eating disorders therapist, one of my supervisors gave me a chilling piece of advice that I never forgot. In a conspiratorial tone she confided, "My primary goal in therapy is to rip daughters away from their mothers." Although I was a young person myself and not yet a mother, this advice filled me with unease. Didn't children need their mothers, and their fathers for that matter? Even though I'd had many conflicts and disagreements with my own mother during adolescence, I still loved and needed her (and still do today!).

The view of my former supervisor is not uncommon. Although I was originally trained to act on the premise that most children develop eating disorders because they have controlling mothers and under-involved fathers, over the years I quickly realized that this is simply not true. Parents of children with eating disorders are generally kind, hard-working, and fair parents who are racked with worry about the health of their child.

Eventually, I followed my instincts and quickly discovered that if I included parents in the treatment process and took into account their astute observations about their child, the information they provided helped me to accelerate their child's recovery. I also realized that in most cases parents had an overwhelming amount of love and dedication to their child's recovery but were lacking the knowledge to put them to the best use. This guide will give you that knowledge plus tools you will need to help your child recover quickly and permanently from her eating disorder.

Note: This is a guide and NOT a substitute for professional eating disorder treatment. It is essential that you use this guide as a tool that will help you secure the BEST treatment for your child as quickly as possible. Most people are not able to recover on their own. Even if your child seems to have ceased the eating disordered behavior, it's likely that this is only temporary and the behaviors will resurface days, months or even years from now. Don't collude with the denial of an eating disorder. It is your job to insist that your child go for help and do your best to secure the highest quality treatment you can within your means.

I have chosen to primarily use the pronoun "she" in this guide to make it easier to read, but boys and men also struggle with eating disorders. This advice applies equally to getting help for your son. There is also a special section on how to help boys with eating disorders.

~ONE~

What Happened To My Child?

The last few days or weeks have possibly been one of your worst nightmares as a parent. Does one of these all-too-common scenarios apply to you?

"My daughter Annie has never been a problem child. She has everything going for her. She is pretty, popular and a straight A student. My husband and I never have to discipline her. We were absolutely shocked when Annie came to us last week and tearfully admitted she has been making herself throw up repeatedly for months. How could everything go from being so right to being so wrong?"

Or:

"Yesterday a small group of our daughter Cecile's friends came over to our house and told us they are really worried about her. They told us that Cecile has been starving herself, skipping lunch at school, and losing too much weight. One of the girls thought she heard Cecile making herself throw up in the school bathroom. We knew she had started dieting and exercising to lose some excess pounds, but we thought this was a positive step and would help her feel better about herself. We confronted Cecile today, but she became extremely angry and denied having a problem. Now what do we do?"

Or:

"Our son Adam has been a member of his school's cross country team since his freshman year. We encouraged him because we felt it was a healthy outlet for him and would help him learn to be part of a team. The first year Adam would only exercise with his team during practice, but over the last year he has become more and more compulsive, going on long runs outside of practice, using the weight room, and doing aerobic exercise videos for hours every day, all while severely limiting the food he eats. He is isolating himself from his friends and doing worse in school. He refuses to cut down on the exercise and won't eat even when we beg him to."

Or:

"Amber, our 12 year old daughter, has gained a lot of weight over the last year and we don't know why. Last week I discovered all kinds of junk food hoarded in her room. When we buy snack foods, we often find them gone the next morning. Her pediatrician suggested we put her on a diet, but it seems the more we restrict her food, the more she 'sneak eats'."

Or:

"A few months ago, when I was cleaning my 15-year-old daughter's room, I found several empty boxes of laxatives and a half-full bottle of diet pills. After confronting her, she admitted to taking these medications daily, and in amounts that far exceed the recommended dose. She said that when she eats foods that are 'bad' for her, she uses the pills so she won't become fat."

It may be hard to believe, but you are definitely not alone. Most of the parents I see in my practice share stories like these. They may have already taken their child to a counselor, who either "just listened" for months while their child continued to throw up, compulsively eat, or starve, or discharged her from therapy, saying kindly, but with exasperation, that "they are not qualified to treat this kind of problem."

Most of the parents I see in treatment are worried to death, afraid to move a muscle because they do not want to make things worse. A well-meaning therapist may have told you to back off and not talk to your child about the eating disorder or food at all, but did not give you any alternatives to help or support your child. This is a HUGE mistake. Your child's eating disorder, as we will see, is a force that has taken over her logic and common sense. Although it is a coping mechanism for her, it is a very dangerous and unhealthy one that could be life threatening. As her parent you MUST get involved, and it is essential that you provide the right kind of support and treatment as soon as possible.

What I have found over the years is that parents, in a desperate attempt to stop their child's eating disordered behaviors, will often impose severe rules and limits that actually sabotage their child's recovery. These rules are imposed out of LOVE, but they are actually destructive. Some examples of rules that do not work for stopping an eating disorder include:

- Monitoring the bathroom so she won't make herself throw up;
- Getting her friends to "report" to you if they see her skipping lunch, purging, or compulsively overeating;
- Keeping certain foods out of the house in an attempt to prevent her from bingeing and/or purging;
- Threatening her with removal of privileges if she does not stop the eating disordered behavior immediately;
- Conversely, offering a reward (monetary, more privileges, a trip, etc.) if she ceases the eating disordered behavior;
- Putting her on a diet program or in a weight-loss camp to help her lose weight.

If you have tried any of these tactics, don't be too hard on yourself. You have done so out of love and concern for your child. Unfortunately, you have most likely found out that these methods either did not work or made things worse. These basic methods might seem to make sense initially, but the magnitude of an eating disorder can easily be underestimated by parents. In other instances, parents are so inundated with an overabundance of opposing information from treatment providers and the internet that they often feel paralyzed about what to do.

For over twenty years I have counseled parents at the end of their rope, who either have tried "everything" to no avail, or who have only just recently found out their child has an eating disorder. Most parents quickly become overwhelmed with all of the advice available, or frustrated by the lack of it. Luckily, there is hope. Once you are equipped with the right information and concrete tools you can use to help your child recover, she will, in most cases, begin to show almost immediate improvement. This Quick Start Recovery Guide for parents will give you the correct information and tools right away to help your child get better fast.

~TWO~

How Do I Know For Sure That My Child Has An Eating Disorder?

Eating disorders are a growing and alarming problem among teenage girls. Girls may chronically overeat, or at the opposite extreme, may starve themselves in an effort to look thin. One common eating disorder—called *anorexia nervosa*—is present when a person diets to the point of losing 25% or more of her normal body weight.

Symptoms of anorexia nervosa

- The person refuses to maintain a minimally normal body weight.

- The person is intensely afraid to gain weight, and the fear is not alleviated by weight loss—it often intensifies.

- There is significant disturbance in the person's perception of the shape or size of his body.

- A girl may lose her period.

- The person achieves weight loss through dieting and food restriction. It usually starts with what the person perceives to be high calorie, or "fattening" foods, but in extreme cases they restrict to very little, or no food.

- Symptoms can include purging (self-induced vomiting) and/or excessive exercise to lose weight.

- Some individuals feel generally overweight, others are overly concerned about certain parts of their bodies. In extreme cases this is called "body dysmorphic disorder"

- Anorexia nervosa can be accompanied by obsessive-compulsive (known as OCD) features: checking, washing, counting, obsessive weighing or measuring of body parts.

- The person's self-esteem is highly dependent upon appearance—any weight gain is seen as a failure or loss of control.

- People with anorexia nervosa are usually high achievers and perfectionists.

- They are usually in denial about the medical dangers of their condition and are often unreliable to provide accurate information about their physical condition or behaviors—in other words, your child may lie to you because she doesn't want to be forced to eat.

Additional facts and statistics

- There is often a history or sexual, physical or verbal abuse (but not always).

- The person may also show symptoms of depression, social withdrawal, irritability, insomnia, and loss of interest in friends and hobbies.

- The possible physical complications of anorexia are numerous and frightening. They include: anemia, blood clots, dehydration, metabolic imbalances from vomiting, low estrogen or testosterone levels, heart arrhythmias, electrolyte imbalances, cold intolerance, dental erosion, lethargy, edema (swelling) during weight gain, impaired kidney function, and osteoporosis.

- Anorexia nervosa is most prevalent in industrialized societies where beauty is associated with thinness; the illness mostly affects Caucasian women, but the percentages are rising in all ethnic groups and among men and boys.

Another common disorder, *bulimia nervosa*, involves a destructive cycle of binging and purging, either by vomiting, the abuse of laxatives or diuretics, or obsessive exercising.

Symptoms of bulimia nervosa

- Repeated episodes of binge eating followed by inappropriate compensatory behaviors such as self-induced vomiting, misuse of laxatives, diuretics, or other medications or supplements, fasting, or excessive exercise.

- People with bulimia are often ashamed of their behaviors and try to hide them, whereas people with anorexia are often in denial that they have a problem.

- Several methods of purging can be used: self-induced vomiting, syrup of ipecac (this is what you administer to people who may have ingested poison in order to induce vomiting), laxatives and diuretics, enemas, fasting and/or excessive exercise.

- The person's self-esteem is closely tied to shape and weight.

- The person is typically within normal weight range, so bulimia is more difficult to discover and more secretive.

Additional facts and statistics:

- There is often a history of sexual, physical or emotional abuse (but not always).

- There are usually also symptoms of depression and anxiety, which can include panic attacks and agoraphobia (extreme anxiety or inability to leave the house).

- One third of those diagnosed with bulimia also abuse drugs and alcohol.

- 90% of people with bulimia are female.

Eating when not hungry, called *emotional eating* or *binge eating*, is another type of eating disorder.

Symptoms of binge eating disorder
- The person eats when under stress and does not pay attention to natural hunger cues.
- The person also can engage in high calorie binges; however, even eating a bite or two of a cookie when not hungry can be classified as a binge.
- The person feels shame and low self-esteem, particularly about eating behavior and body image.
- There is usually an unhealthy cycle of crash diets and binging periods.

Additional facts and statistics:
- Binge eating disorder is common in both women and men.
- These individuals are often taking appetite suppressants and weight control medications prescribed by doctors.
- There is often and overuse/abuse of exercise and body enhancing treatments (plastic surgery, cosmetics, etc.).

Lori Osachy, MSS, LCSW

The following is an article from Skirt Magazine (www.skirt.com) for which Lori was interviewed on Friday, August 27, 2010.

More girls seek plastic surgery
By Tracy Jones

(A) plastic surgeon in Jacksonville, sees it all the time: a 15- or 16-year-old comes in for a consult grasping a picture of Britney Spears or some other celebrity that she wants to look like.

The parents? They're sometimes just along for the ride, and it's the girl who's needling to go under the knife.

"I see them as young as 13 or 14, and I try to put them off and put them off," he said. "As a rule, 18 is kind of my minimum."

(His) patients are just some of many girls in Jacksonville and across the country putting their bodies in the hands of plastic surgeons to fix imperfections and mold their flaws into something they perceive as more beautiful.

According to the American Society of Aesthetic Plastic Surgery, there were 203,308 procedures performed in 2009 on those 18 and under in the United States, compared to 145,094 in 2000. In all age groups, 91 percent of cosmetic procedures were performed on females, reports the American Society of Plastic Surgeons.

Plastic surgery is nothing new. Many women for years elected to have a nip here, a tuck there. While local figures weren't available, there's been an increase nationally in the past five years of plastic surgery among "The Hills"-watching and high school-age demographic, the ASAPS reports.

It's the beauty ideal that some girls try to achieve and the desire to resemble celebrities that worries **Lori Osachy, a psychotherapist who runs the Body Image Counseling Center in Jacksonville.** She said the pressure on young women to meet a model look gives girls the idea that their worth is valued on outward appearances, and the quest for perfection is pushing girls more and more into the waiting rooms of plastic surgery offices.

"Teenage brains are very impulsive, and to make a decision based on impulse and severe pressure from the media and society to look a certain way — it's not a good time in life to make a permanent decision," she said.

She said encouraging girls to set boundaries on who they're friends with and being proud of differences could dissuade their desire for cosmetic surgery, and starting plastic surgery procedures at a young age could start a cycle of a constant need for plastic surgery or manifest into body dysmorphic disorder.

In its 2009 report, the ASPS reported the top five procedures for teens ages 13-19 in order of popularity: nose reshaping, breast reduction in boys, breast augmentation, ear pinning (otoplasty) and liposuction.

They are risks that a number of women, teens or adults, are apparently willing to overlook: Earlier this year, a study by RealSelf.com found 82 percent of women ages 18 to 44 and 80 percent ages 45 to 54 said they would get cosmetic treatments themselves if money weren't an issue. The top-sought surgeries in those age groups were tummy tuck and liposuction.

# # #

Although women are a common target of eating disorders, men and boys are feeling worse about their bodies, too. Research shows many are dieting excessively, over-exercising, and using steroids to achieve a muscular physique. Athletes are particularly vulnerable to these problems. More boys are suffering from eating disorders than is currently assumed, and they often have nowhere to turn for help.

The statistics are frightening and prove that our young men and women stand in the way of lethal danger. Studies suggest that as many as 10% of American youngsters will develop an eating disorder during their teenage years. We also know that between 5% - 20% of the teenagers who develop anorexia or bulimia will ultimately die from their disease. These are staggering quantities of teens. Of those who survive, one in four will continue to suffer these conditions for the rest of their lives.

In light of these statistics, we must remember that **anyone** can develop an eating disorder. They affect people of every socioeconomic level and race, although they are most prevalent among white, upper-middle class females between the ages of 13 and 30. Since teenagers with eating disorders often feel a great deal of shame about their behavior, they rarely seek help from parents, teachers, or other mentors. For this reason it is extremely important for the adults in a young person's life to learn the signs of eating disorders and to learn how to help.

> **Warning signs of eating disorders in girls**
>
> **The following questions represent common signs of eating disorders. If you can answer "yes" to two or more of the following questions, then it is likely your daughter has an eating disorder.**

1. Has she had a large weight loss (25% or more of normal body weight) with no known medical illness causing it?

2. Is she intensely afraid of gaining weight, and does she talk a lot about dieting?

3. Is she eating large amounts of food, which may or may not be followed by vomiting, laxative abuse, unexplained trips to the bathroom, or compulsive exercise?

4. Is she constantly exercising, despite feelings of fatigue and weakness?

5. Is she secretive about dieting, binges, and vomiting?

6. Has there been a noticeable change in her mood with increased proneness to anger, irritability, and depression?

7. Does she have a history of physical, sexual, or emotional abuse?

> **Warning signs of eating disorders in boys**
>
> **The following questions represent common signs of eating disorders. If you can answer "yes" to two or more of the following questions, then it is likely your son has an eating disorder.**

1. Is he preoccupied with the desire to become more muscular and "in shape"?

2. Is he so dissatisfied with parts of his body (such as his chest, waist, stomach, shoulders, or height) that he feels ugly?

3. Does he constantly exercise, despite feelings of fatigue and weakness, and feel extreme guilt when he misses a workout?

4. Does he binge on high calorie foods, and/or purge by vomiting or laxative use?

5. Does he use steroids to increase his muscle mass?

6. Has there been a noticeable change in his mood with increased anger and irritability, or depression?

7. Does he have a history of physical, sexual or emotional abuse?

~Three~

Five Steps To Setting Up The Best Professional Treatment Team

Many parents wonder if professional treatment is absolutely necessary for their child to get well. Eating disorders are mysterious to the average person, and parents often lack full understanding of this complex and dangerous problem. When a person lacks information and guidance about a stressful problem, they can be prone to minimizing it or denying its seriousness. This can unfortunately lead to disastrous consequences. I have spoken to many parents over the years who have insisted that:

"This is just a stage. My son is just experimenting with making himself throw up. It was probably only a few times and he just did it to get attention. Don't all teenagers act out to get noticed?"

Or:

"If we just let this thing run its course, she'll probably grow out of it. All girls try fad diets at this age."

Or:

"We're not going to pay a lot of money for treatment when all she needs to do is eat."

Or:

"We already have a therapist and the doctor on board. A dietitian seems like overkill. We'll add the nutrition part later if we need to."

Eating disorders are illnesses cloaked in secrecy and denial, and this denial is often shared by parents. Do not make the mistake of believing that your child is using her eating disorder to get attention, manipulate you, get in on a temporary fad, or to fit in with her friends. You may believe that if you call her out on the behavior, she'll be able to make the choice to stop.

Eating disorders are not a conscious choice. An eating disorder is a very powerful, subconscious coping mechanism that your child is using to handle extreme pain and stress. Most young people I treat for these problems are models of responsibility and self-control. They are highly perfectionistic and people pleasers. If they could control the eating disorder symptoms, believe me, they would, because they like to control everything else.

Additionally, eating disorders are not like other mental health issues young people face, such as depression or anxiety, which can often be remedied by once-a-week visits to a qualified and empathic therapist. Eating disorders treatment that takes place outside of the hospital or residential setting is known as "outpatient treatment," and treatment occurring inside of a hospital or residential care setting is known as "inpatient treatment." While there are many advantages to inpatient treatment programs, there are also many hidden disadvantages. In fact, sometimes the short-term benefits can turn into long-term detriments.

When a person goes to the hospital for eating disorder treatment, they receive 24/7 support, which includes:

- Psychotherapy several times a week;
- Nutrition counseling several times a week;
- Group therapy every day;
- Visits to the psychiatrist at least once per week;
- Meal planning sessions;
- Meal monitoring;
- Other therapeutic supports such as equine therapy, yoga or body movement therapy, art therapy, etc.

The best inpatient eating disorder treatment programs can truly be lifesavers, as I'll discuss later in this guide. However, there are two major problems that arise:

1) They're extremely expensive, sometimes even if you have health insurance. And if you don't have health insurance, then they are virtually unaffordable.

2) They usually do not adequately prepare the person for going back to REAL LIFE (which for most kids does not consist of daily therapy, meal monitoring, yoga sessions, and not having to go to school!).

So while there are certain advantages to inpatient care, these solutions often serve as a temporary patch to a large, complicated dilemma. The best model for eating disorders treatment that does not take place in a hospital or residential setting is the outpatient team treatment model. This approach essentially mirrors the setup of a hospital program, but allows much more freedom and less disruption of your family's life.

> **TIP: If you choose a top-notch outpatient treatment team from the start, not only will you avoid the disruption and the cost of going to the hospital, you will help your child learn how to cope in a healthy way with the stresses of everyday life.**

The truth is if you secure a quality outpatient treatment team for your child quickly, inpatient treatment is in most cases unnecessary. The emphasis, note, is on "team." If you take your child to only one provider without putting together a team, you are setting her up for failure in her recovery. Strong words, yes, but they're true. Studies show that people with eating disorders have a better prognosis and recover faster when they are working with a treatment team similar to what they would have in a hospital setting. Personally, I will refuse to see a child under 18 for treatment if the parents will not also work with a dietitian and pediatrician. I know that if I don't insist on this the child is probably being set up for failure.

A diagnosis of an eating disorder is not an automatic life sentence of misery for your child. By taking the right steps from the start, she is very likely to recover quickly and permanently (in months, rather than years). However, if you do not get her help, and the right kind, you could be sentencing her to months, or even years, of struggling with an eating disorder. In fact, the younger your child or teen receives quality treatment, the more likely he or she is to recover fully and live a happy and healthy life without being obsessed with food and weight.

> **TIP: Currently, up to 20% of individuals suffering from an eating disorder will do so for the rest of their lives. This staggering statistic would be greatly reduced if the person received the right form of treatment from the start.**

In addition to the comparative cost advantage, there are further benefits of quality outpatient care:

- Your child will usually still be able to attend school, whereas hospitalization will often cause them to have to take incompletes or repeat the year, which further harms their self-esteem;

- You will be creating a team that will always be available in town if your child relapses, so she can get back on track quickly;

- Remember that an inpatient stay is an emergency measure that is most often used to stabilize your child. She still has to learn how to manage the stresses of her life when she leaves the hospital. This is why the most dangerous time for eating disorder patients is immediately after they leave the hospital and return to their regular lives. If there are no supports in place when they return, they are likely to fall back;

- One of the most important therapeutic advantages of using an outpatient treatment team rather than sending your child to a hospital is that you and your child learn how to manage the stresses that triggered the eating disorder in real life. You will be able to practice the techniques that help children recover in your own home, while she is still in school and engaging in her social life.

Who should be on your team?

Ideally, the members of your child's outpatient treatment team should closely mirror those she would have in an inpatient setting. At the bare minimum, the team should consist of your child's pediatrician, a qualified therapist, and a qualified dietitian. Depending on the resources available in your geographic area and your child's specific needs, your team may also include a qualified psychiatrist, a family therapist, a group therapist, your child's school counselor, your child's athletic coach, and/or other adult mentors in your child's life. The role of each person on the treatment team and how often meetings should be with each professional will be outlined in more detail below.

I know you are anxious to find out where to begin, so the following steps are the Parents' Quick Start Recovery Guide. When you follow these five simple steps to procuring the right team for your child, you are taking the best possible steps towards ensuring that your child will make a full recovery fast.

Step 1:
Understand why your child uses an eating disorder and what you can do to help her

Most kids with eating disorders come to me filled with shame and guilt over the fact that they "can't stop" bingeing, purging or starving. In fact, they are extremely successful in most areas of their lives; they are excellent students, attractive, well liked, responsible, and have lots of friends. It is because they are so successful in most areas of their lives that they feel devastated that they just can't "kick" the eating disorder. Does this sound like your child? If you ask a person who binges, purges or compulsively overeats how it feels when they place the food in their mouth, or when they actually purge, they say they may feel guilt or shame right before or after, but DURING the act they feel... release, calm, and relief. I've counseled hundreds of people with eating disorders over the years and they ALL report having these feelings of release during a binge or purge. So even though the eating disordered behaviors seem "crazy," the reason underlying the behavior is healthy and sane! They are after the simple feeling of relief, and their behavior has adapted to pursue this relief in an unhealthy manner. Get ready for the first and most important step in helping your child in her recovery: realizing and truly believing that eating disordered behaviors are actually an attempt by her body to soothe itself, not to destroy itself.

> **TIP: Repeat to yourself: "My child does not lack willpower, she is not lazy, and she is not self-destructive. She is not doing this on purpose and she would stop if she could."**

Finding Help Fast When Your Child or Teen Has an Eating Disorder

An eating disorder is actually the ultimate form of willpower:

An eating disorder is her body's attempt to remove the stress from her life and allow her to continue functioning, albeit at a great risk to her health. Every time your daughter binges, purges, restricts, or compulsively exercises, it's her body trying to tell her that she is under too much stress, telling her in essence: "Hey, you'd better get control of your life or I will." If you and your child do not let go of the shame and guilt surrounding her eating disordered behaviors, she will not be able to recover. The way to let go is to realize that her eating disordered behaviors are, deep down, an attempt to cope with unbearable pain and stress. The behaviors may be destructive, but the motive is healthy and normal.

Knowing your child is not doing these things on purpose, but rather to calm difficult emotions and to alleviate stress will help you to approach her in a more appropriate way. Instead of blaming her for an uncontrollable behavior and pursuing ineffective solutions that exacerbate the problem, you can approach her eating disorder from a more informed perspective. For this reason, any attempt to take the eating disorder away before your child learns better ways of coping is not only futile, but dangerous.

If you try to take your child's eating disordered behaviors from her too quickly, it is like snatching a buoy from a drowning man; he will hold on for dear life so he does not drown! Since an eating disorder arises from deep, subconscious stress factors, you cannot aggressively remove her coping mechanism, or else that stress will work to damage her in other equally destructive ways. In fact, if you don't get to the root of the problem, she is most likely to "switch" unhealthy coping mechanisms. For example, if she is not allowed to purge, she may turn to alcohol use or compulsive exercising to control the stress instead. Keeping this in mind, realize that your child will not be able to go "cold turkey" to give up her eating disorder. As she learns healthier coping mechanisms in treatment, she will be able to go for longer periods of time without purging, starving, bingeing or compulsively exercising. There will, however, be days where the stress is too much for her and she will use these old behaviors to soothe herself.

Regression is part of recovery:

To "regress" during eating disorder treatment means to temporarily exhibit the disordered behavior patterns that you're seeking to resolve. This might mean that if your daughter has been receiving appropriate team treatment for weeks and has seemed to be able to control her habits, those habits might suddenly resurface again. Don't worry – this is actually normal. When parents learn that regression is a normal stage in the recovery process, they are able to keep from panicking, knowing this is not a sign that the treatment is failing.

Finding Help Fast When Your Child or Teen Has an Eating Disorder

What you can do as a parent:

Meanwhile, there are many things you should or should not do at home to provide support during your child's recovery. Now that you understand your child's perspective and dilemma a little bit better, you need to make sure that you are producing an environment inside of your household that gives your child the best chance possible to reach full recovery. You must remember that that you are in a powerful position to help, or hurt, your child's recovery. Here is some useful advice:

What NOT to do at home during your child's recovery:

- Do not try to restrict the eating disordered behaviors by hiding food, locking cabinets, refusing to buy certain foods, standing guard by the bathroom, or interrogating her.

- Do not keep track of how many days she has gone without engaging in the behaviors (this will put too much pressure on your child and causes many children to lie about what they are really doing).

- Do not weigh your child at home – this can be done at the doctor's office. The doctor can even take a "blind weight"; allowing your child to turn around on the scale so she is not stressed by a weight gain.

- Do not become angry if your child "slips" and restricts her food, purges, binges or compulsively exercises.

- Do not make food or appearance a main topic of conversation; focus on feelings instead.
- Do not keep magazines in the house that promote fad diets, crazy beauty routines, or display anorexic looking models in their ads.
- Do not offer rewards or punishments for stopping the eating disordered behaviors (this will just force her to go "underground," making her more resistant to treatment).
- Do not take your child's eating disorder as a personal criticism or a reflection of your parenting skills.
- Do not isolate and insist that the problem must be kept a "secret" from her friends or other family members; telling trusted loved ones is actually a very important step in removing the shame around the eating disorder.
- Do not insist your child eat in order to gain weight, or stop eating as much in order to lose weight; the dietitian will help you learn how to talk to her about food and weight.

What TO DO at home during your child's recovery:

- DO let her know that if she is having a difficult day with the eating disorder, she can come to you and talk about what is stressing her out that day.

- DO express faith that she will be able to learn how to eat according to her natural hunger cues rather than out of emotion.
- DO gently approach her if you think she is having a difficult day and ask her if she would like to talk about what is bothering her.
- DO redirect her if she says she feels fat and ask her if something happened that day that upset her.
- Do read about eating disorders and ask for help and guidance from the treatment team.
- Do express your love and concern for your child, reassuring her that she has what it takes to conquer the eating disorder.
- Do consider yourself an important member of the treatment team; following their suggestions is essential in helping your child get well quickly
- DO buy a variety of foods without focusing on the words "diet," "healthy," "clean," "fattening," or "bad."
- DO encourage your child to stand up for herself and set boundaries with people who may be hurting her.
- DO let her know that as a parent your primary job is to make sure she is safe, healthy and happy, not to be her friend.
- DO consider your own relationship with food and body image, and be brave in facing the hang-ups you may have in these areas.

- DO get her into treatment immediately with the best treatment providers you can find.

- DO take care of yourself; don't put your life totally on hold until your child is better. By taking time out for yourself you are modeling healthy self-care to your child.

You now have Step One under your belt—understanding that your child's eating disorder is a coping mechanism based in a healthy desire for comfort and safety. You also have a list of concrete methods which you can start to use today to positively influence your child in her recovery at home. I will now show you how to create a top-notch support system, or treatment team, that will be the best use of your financial resources and is most likely to help your child permanently recover from her eating disorder.

Lori is interviewed by Tim Jaskiewicz of jax4kids.com in the August 2013 issue:

> Lori Osachy, (LCSW) has helped many teens over the past 15 years with eating disorders, but despite her efforts, she recognizes one disturbing trend. Things are getting worse. Madison Avenue's relentless presentation of the "perfect" body type; teenagers' increasingly complex personal problems; and their exposure to more negative messages about their bodies at a young age are keeping Osachy busier than

ever. She enjoys helping people through her work, but the Jacksonville therapist would gladly welcome a few less phone calls.

"It seems that my patients are getting younger and younger and it's a growing problem among men and boys as well," said Osachy, the Director of The Body Image Counseling Center. "Women are more prone to skewed ideals about body image which they see in the media, but the good news is that you can recover if you receive the right kind of treatment."

Early warning signs parents can watch for include either sudden weight gains or losses in their child without any medical cause; a dramatic change in a child's personality where they appear depressed or withdrawn; a new interest in dieting such as counting calories, skipping meals; and becoming more and more isolated from friends. These might be indications of a larger problem.

Eating disorders manifest themselves in behaviors like anorexia, bulimia, and compulsive overeating. However, these emotional eating habits are driven by mental duress within the young person. Events like a divorce, relocation, or a death in the family are examples of triggers which can lead to body image problems and subsequent eating disorders. Once these problems develop, it's often a challenging task to get a teen to seek treatment. Student athletes, often worried that treatment will prevent them from pursuing their athletic activities, are one such example.

"Some teens will get to the point where they ask for help, but if they don't think they need it, there's a delicate balance between coercion and compromise. I do a lot of parent coaching to inform parents on what they're dealing with and how to best approach their child," added Osachy.

The parents and a therapist can play key roles in assisting a teen with an eating disorder, but a comprehensive approach by a team of professionals has proven to be the most effective way to solve the problem. Doctors can help treat any physical complications, while dietitians can make meal plan recommendations. Psychiatrists can also prescribe medications designed to treat the emotional issues which can be present alongside the body image misconceptions.

In her Jacksonville practice, Osachy hears from parents all too frequently who are overwhelmed by treatment information or lack of it. When your child is sick, everyone knows that life's other priorities take a back seat. "Parents call me every day, desperate to get help, and many of them have wasted a lot of time and money on some of the bad information which is out there," Osachy explained.

Even though problems with food are often byproducts of the mental disorders, Osachy is quick to point out that a solution based on a diet change is not the answer. People move beyond their condition when they feel comfortable about their personal body type and don't compare themselves to unrealistic projections.

"Diets don't work because they don't teach you how to stop your emotional eating. The average size of women in America is size 12, so everyone should feel good about their body type and learn healthy eating habits as a part of the a treatment program," she added.

One day sometime in the future, Lori certainly hopes her phones rings less frequently, but until then, she and others like her do offer solutions which help you and your teenager get through a rough patch.

# # #

Step 2
Take her to the doctor FIRST

The very first thing you must do if you suspect your child has an eating disorder is to make an appointment with her primary doctor. The only way you will know if your child is safe to be in outpatient treatment (i.e. not have to go to an eating disorder treatment center) is to have her pediatrician or primary care physician do a full physical, including the appropriate tests to check for dangerous nutrient imbalances. Waiting to get professional feedback only lengthens the amount of time your child's disorder is hurting her. Taking her to a doctor first demonstrates the seriousness of the problem and your commitment to finding the best solutions as soon as possible.

The doctor will play a very important role in checking your child's weight and overall health while she pursues treatment with the rest of the treatment team you are going to put together for her. The doctor should schedule regular visits, sometimes weekly in cases when a child is seriously underweight, in order to monitor your child's physical health which can deteriorate quickly when eating disorders are present.

If your treatment team were a ship, a qualified pediatrician or doctor must be the captain. A therapist, although essential in helping your child recover, never takes the place of your child's doctor in determining their overall safety. If you have brought your child to a therapist who has not insisted that you set an appointment with the doctor, it is a warning sign that he/she is not qualified to treat eating disorders. Conversely, do not make the mistake of relying solely on the physician for your child's treatment. A doctor should be emotionally supportive, but he/she is not trained in the specific therapeutic treatment techniques that are required for eating disorders recovery. That task should rest on the shoulders of a qualified and licensed therapist.

> **TIP: Don't be afraid to be assertive with doctors and other treatment providers. Most of us grow up learning that doctors are absolute authorities who are not to be questioned. Don't let your fears of questioning authority figures keep you from asking providers perfectly reasonable questions about how, and if, they can help your child. A good doctor, therapist, nutritionist or psychiatrist will answer any and all questions you have about your child, and do so with patience and respect for YOU. If they try to make you feel awkward or ashamed, it's time to look elsewhere!**

Warning signs you have chosen the wrong doctor:

1) He/she does not take a full patient history, including asking about a family history of eating disorders.

2) He/she does not schedule regular follow-up visits to monitor weight, physical complications, and medication checks.

3) He/she threatens your child or uses scare tactics to try to force her to eat, to eat less, to stop compulsively exercising, or to stop purging. It is important to have a primary care physician who is assertive with your child without shaming them. If your child was able to stop on her own, she would have done so already. We have previously discussed how these techniques are not only ineffective, but often make the problem worse. Physicians need to have the expertise to contribute to the solution, not to the problem.

4) He/she is evasive about discussing his/her experience treating eating disorders.

Checklist of questions to ask a pediatrician:

1) How much training and experience do you have treating eating disorders?

2) How serious are my child's symptoms?

3) What tests should my child have to determine if she has any physical problems stemming from the eating disorder?

4) If necessary, how much weight should my child gain, and at what rate?

5) What health complications should we be concerned about, and what can we do to help reverse them?

6) Is inpatient treatment necessary right now, and if not, what changes would cause you to recommend inpatient treatment?

7) If my daughter has lost her period due to the eating disorder, will it return, and when?

8) If you do not have experience with eating disorders treatment, can you refer me to another doctor who has?

9) What are your thoughts about using psychiatric medicine as a part of my child's recovery? What side effects should I be aware of if we use them?

10) Can you refer me to a counselor and a dietitian who specialize in eating disorders? Will you be willing to communicate regularly with them, including them in the treatment plan?

Step 3
How to find a QUALIFIED eating disorder therapist

After you identify the right doctor to be the leader of your outpatient treatment team, it is time to add the rest of the team members. A doctor focuses on the physical aspects of an eating disorder and is qualified to tell you about your child's current and projected health. But other professionals need to be brought alongside to tend to your child's emotional health. That's where an eating disorder therapist comes in.

> **NOTE:** I will be using the terms *therapist* and *counselor* interchangeably in this guide. Keep in mind that there are people who may call themselves counselors, therapists, coaches or treatment specialists but are not licensed by their state to do so. Make sure you ask if the therapist has a license and if it is current. Do not take your child to someone who is not adequately licensed and trained to practice psychotherapy.

So many of the parents I have worked with wasted months or years of time and money having their child work with a therapist who was not qualified to successfully treat eating disorders. Selecting qualified healthcare providers to help your child is **the single most important task you will perform in this process** and can mean the difference between full recovery or years of unnecessary suffering. But how do you find the right therapist when you have to consider cost, geographic location, lack of knowledge about the correct approach to treatment, and other issues? Here are guidelines that will help you find the right therapist as quickly as possible the first time you try:

- First ask the physician for his/her recommendation for a therapist. Usually they have worked with qualified counselors before and will save you a load of searching.

- You can also use the following websites to find therapists in your geographic area:

    www.anad.org

    www.edreferral.com

    www.neda.com

    www.bulimia.com

    www.4eatingdisorders.com

The therapists listed on these sites have had to demonstrate a basic level of proficiency and experience with eating disorders treatment. The websites will often list a therapist's fees, if they offer a sliding fee scale, and which insurances, if any, they accept. All of this information makes these resources excellent places to find that ideal therapist for your child. Once you have chosen a therapist, she will be able to suggest other members that should be a part of the treatment team. As she gets to know you and your child, she may suggest talking to your child's athletic coach, youth leader, or a trusted teacher who can also help to support her recovery. She may also suggest that your child participate in group therapy with other young people who have eating disorders. Sometimes these groups are not available in town, but if they are, participation has been repeatedly proven to accelerate recovery.

Typically, the therapist will need to see your child once or twice a week in the beginning, depending on how severe her symptoms are. When the symptoms have dissipated, she will not have to come as often, usually once or twice a month, then for occasional follow-up visits to check on her progress. I tell my patients that they should expect the typical course of treatment to be three to six months, and sometimes up to one year or more in severe cases, but this is rare.

> **TIP: Make sure to ask for your child's input when interviewing and selecting qualified treatment providers. It is important that she feel comfortable with and supported by the treatment team. Just because you feel comfortable with the person does not necessarily mean your child will. Don't be afraid to ask how a potential provider works with children as opposed to adults (the approach can be quite different in order to gain trust). Having said that, keep in mind that many children are afraid to give up their eating disordered behavior at first and can be resistant to treatment even with the most kind, qualified and supportive professionals. A good rule of thumb is to observe whether your child feels uncomfortable with everyone you have interviewed, or just with one or two people. In the latter case, it will help build trust between you and your child to address her concerns and allow her to meet with additional candidates.**

Finding Help Fast When Your Child or Teen Has an Eating Disorder

Warning signs you have chosen the wrong therapist:

1) The therapist cannot give a concrete, scientifically-based treatment plan for your child, or does not outline a plan at all.

2) The therapist excludes you from treatment, reassuring you that she and your child need to work together privately.

3) The therapist subtly or overtly makes you feel as if it is your fault, implying that your lack of parenting skills has caused the disorder. Or they blame your child, trying to guilt them into stopping the eating disordered behaviors "cold turkey."

4) The therapist tells you that your child can never fully recover from an eating disorder because it's an addiction.

5) Weeks or months go by without communication from the therapist, and your child does not seem to be improving, or seems to be getting even worse. (Unfortunately, this happens all the time, and is very dangerous for your child).

6) The therapist is either adamantly for OR against the use of psychiatric medicine for eating disorder treatment. (Each child is different, needing a specialized treatment plan that may or may not include use of medications).

7) The therapist assures you that he can do the nutrition counseling along with the therapy, so a dietitian is unnecessary.

8) The therapist talks about her own weight or body image issues with your child.

Question checklist to ask a potential therapist:

1) How much training and experience do you have treating eating disorders?

2) What is your basic approach and techniques for treatment? Will they be easy for my child to understand and use?

3) How long can we expect treatment to last before we see our child start to improve?

4) How long and how frequent are the treatment sessions?

5) Do you accept health insurance and/or offer a sliding fee scale or discount package?

6) Will you include us as part of the treatment team, and how often?

7) How are you going to address the eating disorder symptoms right away in order to help my child regain her physical health?

8) What are your thoughts on use of medication?

9) Will you be working with a dietitian who is an eating disorder specialist, along with my child's pediatrician and psychiatrist?

10) How many eating disorder patients have you treated over the last two years, and how many of them have recovered fully? What is your definition of full recovery?

11) Do you have any complaints against you?

Step 4
How to find a QUALIFIED nutritionist/dietitian

A common and costly mistake that people with eating disorders make is to see a therapist without including a nutritionist on the treatment team or vice versa. Hiring just a therapist OR a nutritionist to treat an eating disorder is like trying to row a boat with one oar – you may eventually get where you want to go, but it will take a lot longer and you will probably end up going in circles. A therapist is not trained in nutrition, and a nutritionist is not trained to be a therapist. One cannot be substituted for the other, and we are ethically and legally bound NOT to provide counsel in the other's area of expertise.

If you are seeing a nutritionist who does not also refer you to a therapist, or a therapist who tells you they can provide the nutritional counseling even though they are not a licensed dietitian (I wish I could say I have not seen this happen, but it does all the time), it is time to start over and find a more qualified treatment team. Additionally, not all nutritionists are created equally. Many dietitians do not have any experience treating eating disorders, and this requires a very separate skill set. Be assertive when interviewing a nutritionist, just as you were with the physician and therapist. And of course, make sure that the dietitian is fully licensed within your state, and that her license is current.

A common question I receive about nutrition counseling is, "I already know a lot about nutrition and what is healthy eating and what is not. Why should I pay someone just to tell me what I already know?" Even though you may already know a lot about nutrition, the way you implement that knowledge is subject to the many distorted messages society bombards us with every day about what constitutes healthy eating and weight. Additionally, a qualified eating disorder nutrition specialist will address those distorted thoughts and fears your child has about his body, weight and eating habits, and help him to overcome them. A nutritionist does much more than tell you what foods are good and bad to eat – they provide professional, comprehensive treatment regarding eating habits, working to educate and heal your child.

> **TIP: Don't skimp on treatment by hiring a nutritionist/dietitian who is not an eating disorder specialist, or by not hiring a dietitian at all; you and your child will pay more financially and emotionally in the long run.**

Competent nutrition therapists should involve the client in a discussion of the following topics, listed at **www.healthyplace.com.**

- What kind and how much food the client's body needs;
- Symptoms of starvation and of refeeding (the process of beginning to eat normally after a period of starvation);

- Effects of fat and protein deficiency;
- Effects of laxative and diuretic abuse;
- Metabolic rate and the effect of restricting, bingeing, purging, and yo-yo dieting;
- Food facts and fallacies;
- How restricting, bingeing, and taking laxatives or diuretics influence hydration (water) shifts in the body and thus body weight on the scale;
- The relationship between diet and exercise;
- The relationship of diet to osteoporosis and other medical conditions;
- The extra nutritional needs during certain conditions such as pregnancy or illness;
- The difference between "physical" and "emotional" hunger;
- Hunger and fullness signals;
- How to maintain weight;
- Establishing a goal weight range;
- How to feel comfortable eating in social settings;
- How to shop and cook for self and/or significant others;
- Nutritional supplement requirements.

You can use these websites to find competent nutritionists in your geographic area:

www.intuitiveeating.org
www.anad.org
www.edreferral.com

www.neda.com
www.bulimia.com
www.4eatingdisorders.com

As with the therapist, your child will need to see the nutritionist once a week in the beginning, depending on how severe her symptoms are. When the symptoms have dissipated, she will not have to come as often, usually once or twice a month, then for occasional follow-up visits to check on her progress.

> **TIP: Here is another piece of advice I give to all parents searching for the best treatment team providers: "Hiring a therapist (or a doctor, nutritionist, or psychiatrist) is like buying a pair of shoes. If you try a pair on and they do not fit, do you pay for them and wear them out of the store? No! You try on more shoes until you find THE BEST pair. The same goes for hiring health care providers. If the fit doesn't feel right, keep interviewing! You don't have to buy the first pair of shoes you try on. Remember the saying, "A chain is only as strong as its weakest link"? You cannot afford to have even one weak link in your child's treatment team. The stronger the links, the faster and more successful her recovery will be. If you receive good recommendations as outlined below, it should only take you a few weeks or less to shop around and find the right providers.**

Warning signs you have chosen the wrong dietitian:

1) If she says, "I have counseled a few people with eating disorders before, so I think we should be OK," or "I don't primarily work with eating disorders, but I'd like to try and help." Keep searching.

2) If he tries to put your child on a restrictive diet, such as one that denies your child certain foods or food groups (i.e. no white sugar or carbs, no dessert foods allowed in the house). You want to choose a nutritionist who follows a non-diet approach, encouraging your child to eat all foods in moderation, and to learn to obey her internal hunger cues without dieting.

3) If she doesn't recommend that your child sees her doctor regularly to determine if she is safe to be in outpatient treatment.

4) If the nutritionist assures you that she can do the counseling along with nutrition, so a therapist is unnecessary.

5) If the nutritionist does not ask to speak with you on a regular basis to work with you on how to help your child with her progress at home.

Checklist of questions to ask a dietitian:

1) Have you ever worked with eating disorders?

2) How long have you worked with eating disorder patients?

3) In what settings have you worked with eating disorder patients? (i.e. in private practice, in a hospital, in an outpatient program?)

4) Will you collaborate with my child's other healthcare providers on a regular basis?

5) What is your treatment philosophy for nutrition counseling, and especially for treating eating disorders?

6) How many eating disorder patients have you treated over the last two years, and how many of them have recovered fully? What is your definition of full recovery?

7) How are you going to address the eating disorder symptoms right away in order to help my child regain her physical health?

8) Is it your standard practice to work with a therapist who is an eating disorder specialist, along with my child's pediatrician and psychiatrist?

9) Do you accept health insurance and/or offer a sliding fee scale or discount package?

10) Do you have any complaints against you?

Step
How to find a QUALIFIED psychiatrist

There is a huge stigma in our culture about seeing a therapist, and it becomes worse when the possibility of having to see a psychiatrist is added to the mix. It's no wonder, then, that when I gently mention to parents that their child may need to see a psychiatrist, the look of horror and dread that comes to their faces. A psychiatrist is a trained medical doctor who specializes in prescribing psychiatric medicines. Some psychiatrists also provide counseling. Parents have a lot of fears about putting their child on psychiatric medicines, including:

- My child's personality will change; she'll become like a "zombie;"
- The side effects will be dangerous – I've heard reports that some teens become suicidal on these medicines;
- The medicine will cause my child to become "addicted" and he will be more susceptible to using illegal drugs;
- She'll rely on the medicine forever and won't learn how to solve her own problems;
- Use of the medicine will go on her "permanent record" and could ruin her chances to get into a good college or find a job.

I am going to tell you what I tell all the parents I work with, some people are able to recover from eating disorders without the use of psychiatric medications, but most are not. I have seen kids suffer unnecessarily because their parents were too afraid to try medication that would help ease the stress that comes with trying to change eating disordered behaviors.

As for the fears outlined above, here are the reassurances I provide:

- In very rare cases, an individual will become MORE depressed and lethargic on a prescribed psychiatric medicine. As long your child is seeing a therapist and psychiatrist that you trust, you can be reassured that they will very closely monitor her response to the medication. Also know that it is impossible for medications to change one's personality, which lies in your genetics. You should also consider that it is the EATING DISORDER stealing your child's personality and happiness, not the medications prescribed to help her.

- Again, in very rare cases, psych meds have caused suicidal thinking in adults and teenagers. To put this in perspective, I have been a therapist for over twenty years and have seen hundreds of patients. I can only recall only TWO times when a patient who was prescribed medicine became so depressed they felt suicidal, and we caught it immediately and asked the psychiatrist to change the medicine or remove the medicine entirely. Compare this with the HUNDREDS of children and teens I've treated who got better quickly in part because they were put on medicine. Most of these kids were also able to go off the medicine within 1-2 years.

- Not all drugs are addictive, and most of the medicines outlined below fall into that category. In reality, an untreated eating disorder is more likely to lead drug and alcohol use than being prescribed psychiatric medicine. This is because eating disordered behavior is used to soothe stress in the same way as drugs and alcohol. In fact, many patients I see with eating disorders are either already abusing drugs or alcohol, or have a history of it. While your child is on the prescribed medications, she will be learning alternative coping mechanisms that are much healthier for her, and these techniques will actually insulate her from future drug abuse.

- As I mentioned above, most of the people I counsel only stay on medicine for 1-2 years or less. The therapy helps them to develop healthy, drug-free, coping mechanisms that they can use in times of stress for the rest of their lives. Although a small number of people stay on medication for longer periods of time, the goal is almost always to live medication free. If your child is suffering from severe depression or anxiety, or is exhausted by constant purging, she will not have the emotional or cognitive energy to successfully complete the therapy. Medicine, properly prescribed and monitored, can be essential in alleviating these symptoms so she can fully participate in treatment.

- I have never seen a child not be accepted to college or lose a job because she was on medicine. You also have to consider all of the students who have to leave school because their eating disorder symptoms prevent them from being able to study effectively and to be involved socially with their friends. Receiving the right medication could be what gets them into college, not what keeps them out of it.

Just as therapists are not allowed to counsel about nutrition, we are not allowed to prescribe or even recommend medications to a patient. But we CAN discuss the research with parents, and the research shows unequivocally that medicines can ease eating disorder symptoms quickly, leading to a faster recovery time.

Medications used in the treatment of eating disorders typically include:

- **Selective serotonin reuptake inhibitors (SSRIs)**—the preferred type of antidepressant, thought to help decrease the depressive symptoms often associated with some eating disorders, i.e. Fluoxetine (Prozac)

- **Tricyclics (TCAs)**—another type of antidepressant thought to help with depression and body image. TCAs are generally only used if SSRIs treatments fail. i.e. Desipramine (Norpramin)

- **Antiemetics**—drugs specifically designed to suppress nausea or vomiting. i.e. Ondansetron (Zofran)

- **Anticonvulsants**—the drug Topomax, usually prescribed for epilepsy and other seizure disorders, has been found to help some eating disorders patients control their bingeing and purging significantly because of its appetite controlling side effects.

- **Atypical antipsychotics**—the drug Olanzapine (marketed under the name Zyprexa) has been shown in some anorexic patients to increase appetite and food intake.

A psychiatrist will see your child for a thorough assessment appointment, which could take up to an hour. He will then prescribe medications he feels will be helpful in easing your child's obsessive worrying about food, and any underlying mental health issues such as anxiety and depression. Usually these medications take from 4-6 weeks to take full effect, so it's normal if he asks to see you back in a month or more. At that time he will either adjust the medications, or instruct you to continue them as prescribed. Once-a-month visits are usually adequate from that point on.

Warning signs you have chosen the wrong psychiatrist:

1) The psychiatrist is evasive about his or her experience treating eating disorders, or tries to assure you that he can help your child despite his inexperience.

2) The psychiatrist has difficulty emotionally connecting with you and/or your child and helping you to feel reassured.

3) He or she minimizes your concerns about putting your child on medications, or seems annoyed to answer your questions.

4) Your child has been seeing the psychiatrist for two to three months and does not seem to be improving, or the psychiatrist sees your child alone repeatedly without giving you an update on her response to the medicine(s).

5) The appointments seem brief, rushed, or superficial, and you feel pressured to leave before your questions or concerns are fully addressed.

Checklist of questions to ask a psychiatrist:

1) How much training and experience do you have treating eating disorders?

2) How serious are my child's symptoms?

3) What tests should my child have to determine if she has any psychiatric problems stemming from or causing the eating disorder?

4) What health complications or side effects should we be concerned about from the medications you prescribe, and what can we do to help minimize them?

5) Is inpatient treatment necessary right now, and if not, what changes would cause you to recommend inpatient treatment?

6) If you do not have experience with eating disorders treatment, can you refer me to another psychiatrist who has?

7) What are your thoughts about using psychiatric medicine as a part of my child's recovery?

8) Can you refer me to a counselor and a dietitian who specialize in eating disorders? Will you be willing to communicate regularly with them, including them in the treatment plan?

9) How long do you estimate my child will need to use medications? Do you have a plan for helping my child get off the medicine once she is in recovery?

10) Are there any complaints filed against you?

Remember the statistic I shared earlier that **20% of people with eating disorders will never seek help or die from complications of eating disorders?** It is my goal to help your child avoid becoming one of the 20%. If I didn't help people recover successfully from the emotional and physical devastation of eating disorders every day, I wouldn't be doing the work I do. Your child CAN recover from an eating disorder quickly and permanently. By taking action as soon as possible and following the five step quick start guide, you will be taking one enormous step towards placing your child in the 80% who leave an eating disorder behind them forever.

Know that above all else, an eating disorder is not a natural state, and your child, no matter the age or gender, is well within reach of receiving the help needed to appropriately treat them and return them to health. Have hope. In this guide I have covered five integral steps in securing the best help for your child fast. The first step is changing your mindset as a parent about the eating disordered behavior. Realizing that it is not an attempt for your child to act out or get attention, and is, for now, beyond her control to stop will help you to be more patient and supportive. Just as important, being reassured that recovery can be quick and permanent will soothe your fears and move you from a place of hopelessness and fear to a place of positive action.

Steps 2-5 gave specific guidance and action steps about how to swiftly put together a skilled treatment team to help your child let go of her eating disordered behaviors once and for all. Be aware of your own internal alarm system when you review the warning signs. If you believe you may have chosen an inappropriate treatment provider, have courage to continue looking until you feel satisfied with your choices. Don't forget to take care of yourself in the process, and seek out extra support from a therapist coach if need be.

Remember that with the right perspective, knowledge, and team, your child will be provided with the essential network of support that can heal them. The inundation of media and peer pressure can easily cause our impressionable children to fall into the trap of an eating disorder. But they don't have to stay there. If you're reading this eBook, it's because you love your child and greatly desire to know what you can do to help her. Now that you know what to do, the responsibility rests in your hands to take action. So, keep loving your child and work toward forming the outpatient treatment team you know will provide them with the help they need.

~Four~

Parent FAQs

Q: We feel uncomfortable questioning doctors about their qualifications and background. Isn't this inappropriate and disrespectful to them?

Absolutely not, as long as you ask them in a polite but firm manner. Putting it bluntly, hiring a doctor or therapist should be treated the same way as hiring someone to paint your house. Do you choose the first painter you call, or do you ask him about his qualifications (i.e. How many houses has he painted before? Has he had experience painting your type of molding? Has he ever been fired from a painting job before? How long will it take him to paint the house?). If he were disrespectful to you when you asked these questions, or pressured you to hire him before you were reassured or had proof he was qualified, would you go ahead and sign the contract? Additionally, if he does an awful job, or doesn't do it within the time specified, or lies about his qualifications; you would fire him right away, wouldn't you? If you are willing to ask these questions and set these limits with a house painter, why wouldn't you with your child's treatment providers?

Medical professionals in our society are assumed to be absolute authorities just by the nature of their titles, and the average person feels since they are not trained or an expert, they are not justified to ask about experience and qualifications. As parents, you must get over this anxiety and realize that you are trying to HIRE the best professionals to treat your child. How can you do this if you are unwilling to ask them pointed questions on their skill and expertise?

If you have never seen a therapist before, it can feel uncomfortable and difficult to ask them about their qualifications and treatment approach, but it is very important that you do so. A good therapist will not make you feel ashamed or stupid for questioning them about your child's treatment; in fact, they should welcome your questions and concerns and in some cases offer you a session alone in order to answer them.

> **TIP: Before you make an appointment with a potential treatment provider, have a list of questions ready that you can ask them by phone (refer to the lists provided above for help). Be aware if the person rushes you off the phone, seems annoyed, or does not have specific answers to your questions.**

Q: What if our insurance does not cover any of the qualified and recommended therapists?

This is a dilemma that many parents face as they try to secure the very best treatment for their child. Unfortunately, the hard truth is that most of the most qualified therapists have removed themselves from insurance panels because the insurance companies do not pay them well enough and do not cover enough treatment sessions to support full recovery of your child.

It may seem tempting to use a therapist that is covered under the insurance but is not fully qualified, but you will end up paying more financially and emotionally in the end if your child does not receive proper treatment. In fact, a bad experience could turn your child off to therapy and keep her from asking for help and support in the future if her eating disorder gets worse.

Private pay rates may seem out of reach, but if you compare them to the cost of inpatient care, which is also rarely covered by insurance, it is MUCH less by comparison.

On the following page is an example in hard numbers:

Cost of an outpatient treatment team:

Weekly doctor visits for overall health checks	$25 copay
Two weekly visits to qualified therapist for individual and/or family therapy	$300 ($150/hour average)
One weekly visit to a qualified nutritionist	$150/hour
One monthly visit to qualified psychiatrist for med prescription and med check	$25 copay
One weekly group therapy visit	$40/session

Total: $540/week for an average of three months to show significant improvement comes to $6480. At six months the cost is $12,960.

This is a lot of money. But when you consider how much inpatient treatment costs, you'll see that you are getting the best possible care at a comparatively affordable rate. "Treatment of an eating disorder in the US ranges from **$500 per day to $2,000 per day. The average cost for a month of inpatient treatment is $30,000.** It is estimated that individuals with eating disorders need anywhere from 3 – 6 months of inpatient care. Health insurance companies for several reasons do not typically cover the cost of treating eating disorders." (Statistics taken from **http://www.state.sc.us/dmh/anorexia/statistics.htm).**

> **TIP:** Call your insurance company and ask if they provide partial reimbursement if you use a therapist that is a specialist but out-of-network. If there are no eating disorder specialists listed on your insurance company's list of providers, ask if they will create a single case agreement that will pay for the treatment sessions.

In addition to the comparative cost advantage, remember the additional treatment benefits to pursuing outpatient care that I described at the beginning of the guide. Add to these the following economic benefits:

- You do not have to pay for accommodations and travel to the inpatient hospital, which is unlikely to be located in your town;
- Many private pay therapists offer sliding fee scales and discount counseling packages that can help with the cost;
- Using eating disorder specialists now will save you money in the long-term because you will not have to spend money later trying to make up for unsuccessful "discount" treatment now;
- The overall cost of the most conservative estimate of recovery time (i.e. most of my patients, not all, but most, are stabilized within three months of beginning treatment and do not require two times, or even one time per week counseling at that point) is still **LESS THAN HALF** of the cost of inpatient care.

> **TIP: If your child needs a higher level of care than an outpatient treatment team can provide, but you cannot afford the hospital fees, consider placing her in what is called an "intensive outpatient treatment program." In these types of programs, your child sleeps at home every night, but goes for treatment at the hospital or residential setting during the day. These programs can be a lot less costly than inpatient care, and provide daily support.**

Q: What if there are no qualified eating disorder treatment professionals in my area?

This situation is all too common. Most eating disorder professionals are located in large metropolitan areas. Luckily, new technology can make it easier to access treatment out-of-town. For example, many of my patients do not live in my town. They talk to me using Skype or Facetime. If you have never used these programs to be able to view the person you are talking to, consider giving them a try. Although some of my clients do not prefer it, most feel like they are right in the room with me, and technology is improving every day. I also counsel clients over the phone. You can speak remotely with therapists and nutritionists, but need to be able to physically visit a doctor or psychiatrist. In general, face-to-face with a qualified professional is best, and if your commute to their office is less than two hours away, then you should travel to see them.

> **TIP: Make sure if you are using a therapist or dietitian remotely (through Skype, phone or Facetime), that your insurance will cover the sessions; be prepared to find that most insurance companies do not.**

You can Skype or do phone consults with the right nutritionist if they are not located in your town. One of the nutritionists I work with in my practice is located in a different city, so my patients have regular Skype sessions with her. What I tell them is that it's better for your child to have a remote session with someone who is the best at what they do, rather than sit face-to-face with someone who can't help.

> **TIP: Make sure that the therapist is licensed to treat your child in your geographic area. Many mental health licenses only allow you to treat people from out of state if they physically come to your office. However, the opposite is also true. If your legal residence is in the same state as the therapist, they can continue to counsel you by phone or Skype if you leave the state. This is how I am able to counsel college students all over the country. (continued next page)**

> **They begin treatment with me in high school, and are still legal residents of Florida while in college, so I can continue to provide them support wherever they go. My strong advice is to either travel to a qualified therapist if the commute is less than two hours, or use remote counseling tools rather than see someone in town who is unqualified.**

Q: When is hospitalization necessary?

Most situations will not require hospitalization if you set up the proper treatment team quickly. However, there are definitely situations when a hospital stay is required. If your child is dangerously low weight and has physical symptoms which require stabilization, such as low heart rate, fainting, heart palpitations, or low potassium levels, then hospitalization is necessary. This is another important reason why it is ESSENTIAL to involve your child's doctor from the start. The reason I keep repeating this is that I have seen too many children walk into my office at a dangerously low weight only to find out they have been seeing an unqualified therapist for months or YEARS who allowed them to remain in treatment without getting a medical checkup. Eating disorders are illnesses of denial, and this denial can extend to inexperienced treatment providers.

We see the need for hospitalization most commonly in people who are anorexic rather than bulimic, or compulsive overeaters. Anorexia is the most difficult of the eating disorders to treat because the more weight the person drops, the FATTER they feel, and the more fearful they are to eat. Combined with the fact that severe anorexia results in loss of natural hunger cues, it becomes close to impossible for the child to re-feed to a healthy weight. In this situation, the hospital or residential treatment program can truly be a lifesaver. It provides support and supervision to allow your child to re-feed steadily, helping them to handle the overwhelming anxiety that comes with this task. As the person's weight stabilizes, they become more rational and capable of following a meal plan once they are discharged to outpatient treatment.

Q: What if my child refuses to go for counseling?

Many parents find themselves in a situation where they know their son or daughter desperately needs help for an eating disorder, but cannot convince them to go for treatment. I must reemphasize that an eating disorder is a powerful illness that becomes a strong voice in your child's mind convincing them that they must continue bingeing, purging, starving, and/or compulsively exercising at all costs. Your child is using these behaviors to feel in control and secure, so some kids will rebel towards letting them go. The most important thing to remember when your child is refusing treatment is that **you are not your child's friend but you are her protector.**

You must let her know that although you love her very much, you are responsible for her health and safety and must insist on putting strong consequences in place if she does not comply with treatment. It may not be enough to insist that she go for help. In these cases, use of a behavior contract can be very helpful to "convince" defiant children to engage in treatment. For example, if your child is an athlete, you can firmly let him know that he will not be allowed to continue in his sport until he is going to all medical appointments regularly and until his doctor, therapist, and nutritionist give the OK to resume physical activity. Remember that these approaches should only be used to push your child to see the professionals; they should never be used to try to alter their eating disordered behavior.

I have also, for example, counseled parents to let their 17-year-old know that she will not be allowed to attend college in the fall until the same circumstances are met. Your child will likely cry, complain, or become angry when you set these rules, but underneath, she will be relieved that you are taking charge and helping her get well. I often advise parents to seek counseling themselves to receive support and encouragement not to give in to a child's pleas to forego treatment. When your child is out of the grip of the eating disorder, she will forgive you.

Q: What if my child is over 18 years old and refuses treatment, even though we know she is in trouble?

It is more difficult, but not impossible, to force an adult child to enter treatment. If your child is dependent at all on you financially (i.e. for college costs, car or rent payments, etc.), you can use these dependencies as leverage. Having said that, **you should never withdraw love or emotional support to force a child into counseling.** For example, you should never say something like, "Dad and I do not want to have contact with you until you go to treatment." Even if you do not have financial leverage over your child, don't give up on encouraging them to seek treatment. List the evidence you see to her as clearly as you can to help her avoid denial. For example, instead of saying, "You seem like you never want to eat," try "You haven't sat down to eat dinner with us in the last several months," or "Your dad and I have noticed that you've lost an alarming amount of weight recently, and we're worried about you." Make sure you have ready a list of top notch health care providers and their contact numbers, so when the person you love is ready, you can get them in for counseling right away before they change their mind.

Also, consider having several appointments alone with a therapist who is an eating disorders treatment specialist to receive coaching and support in setting limits and following through with your resistant older child. I often counsel parents whose child I have never met, but am still able to help them "convince" their child to get treatment.

Q: My child is an athlete. Are there any special considerations I should keep in mind?

Throughout the years, many famous athletes have admitted that they suffered with an eating disorder for years before they sought help. Famous gymnasts, such as Kathy Johnson, Nadia Comanceci and Cathy Rigby admitted to fighting eating disorders. Rigby, a 1972 Olympian, battled anorexia and bulimia for 12 years. She went into cardiac arrest on two occasions because of it. Christy Henrich, one of the world's top gymnasts, died in 1994 from multiple organ failure from extreme anorexia and bulimia. More recently, Amanda Beard, Olympic swimming champion, published an autobiography that described her lifetime struggle with bulimia. Certain sports are more prone to eating disordered behaviors than others.

Female athletes are especially at risk in sports which emphasize a thin body or appearance, such as gymnastics, ballet/dance, figure skating, swimming, distance running, horse racing, and horse riding. Male athletes are especially at risk in wrestling, body building, long distance running and other sports that require "making weight." There are many reasons why athletic kids can be more prone to eating disorders than their nonathletic peers, including pressures within the sport to be fit and thin, judges rewarding thinner athletes, and coaches pressuring them to be thin by criticizing their bodies or weight. For example, consider that in 1976 the average gymnast was 5'3" weighing 105 pounds; in 1992 the average gymnast was 4'9" weighing 88 pounds.

There is also a widespread and unsubstantiated belief that lower body fat enhances performance. Additionally, individuals who are preoccupied with weight and appearance may be more likely to participate in athletics. A dramatic increase in exercise can cause a decrease in appetite and severe weight loss. Some or all of these risk factors can combine to create a "perfect storm" for developing an eating problem.

Athletes at risk for eating disorders are often those who are particularly anxious and critical of their own athletic performance and who express these concerns by dissatisfaction with their bodies. Make sure to look for these signs for eating disorders in your young athlete:

- fatigue;
- weakness;
- lightheadedness;
- broken bones;
- leg cramps;
- irregular heart rate;
- In girls, watch for what medical professionals call "the female athlete triad": amenorrhea (loss of menstrual period), disordered eating, and osteoporosis (brittle bones).

> **TIP: Be aware that athletes are often aware of the symptoms of eating disorders, but do not want to acknowledge them for fear they will be required to stop their sport. Except for extreme cases, reassure your child that she will not only be able to continue in her sport, but will improve her performance if she is eating and taking care of her body properly.**

Young athletes are usually motivated to get better so that they can continue their sport. Make it clear that her eating disordered behavior hurts her performance rather than enhances it. With proper education and a reassurance that their performance will actually improve with recovery and that they are unlikely to become overweight, your child athlete is likely to get better faster. Remember that this type of support can best be provided by a team of professionals that also includes you.

Q: How do I help my child feel better about her body image and weight when she lives in a society obsessed with dieting?

Last year I saw a story on Good Morning America about a married couple whose job is to scout for potential supermodels. The story featured three teenage girls (ALL already painfully thin, I may add) who were "discovered" by this pair. The agents were proud to disclose their regimen for transforming the teens into supermodel material. First, they are put on a "bare bones diet" of "lettuce, carrots and egg whites." Then they are expected to "train like professional athletes," using the treadmill up to 10 miles per day. One of the teens was actually filmed pleading, "Feed me!" (Check out the full story at **http://abcnews.go.com/GMA/video/models-made-14516782.**)

When was the last time you saw a professional athlete eating only lettuce, carrots and egg whites? Michael Phelps eats a 12,000 calorie/day diet when training for the Olympics. Girls then see these supermodels, hear about their "lettuce, carrots, and egg whites" diet, and begin to adopt the same eat-very-little-and-exercise-too-much regimen. These habits result, not in the girls becoming supermodels; they result in the girls developing eating disorders. Another not-so-surprising fact is that the modeling industry is notorious for having an astronomical number of members with eating disorders. These twisted notions of what beauty is and how to achieve it need to be counteracted with healthy lifestyle knowledge.

In my psychotherapy practice I have had the opportunity over the years to talk intimately with hundreds of women and girls about how they feel about their bodies. What I've found is that, with the right kind of help, recovery from years of debilitating eating disorder symptoms is often relatively quick, but body hatred is much harder to eradicate. A study done by the November 12, 2011 issue of Oprah magazine drove home this point. They compared women in their early sixties and girls in their late teens to find out how body image changes (or not) over the life span. When asked "Do you think you have a healthy body image?" 62.1% of the 60+ year olds said yes, compared to 56.8% of teens. Could it really be true that body image improves less than 6% over the course of 40 years?

It's no wonder when we consider the way the mainstream media bombards women and girls with unrealistic images of the "ideal woman." Case in point—Brittany Spears participated in an article for *Marie Claire* where she allowed the magazine to place her original pictures next to the final airbrushed ads. Take a look at **http://www.marieclaire.co.uk/news/beauty/450528/pics-before-after-britney-s-airbrushed-candie-s-ads.html.** The comparison is astonishing—wrinkles and blemishes have disappeared, legs, waist and derriere slimmed several sizes—all with a few clicks of a mouse. The more daughters see of the idealized, unrealistic versions of a woman's figure, the more they compare these versions to their own real shapes. And just as these PhotoShopped pictures present unrealistic standards, so too, do girls begin to attempt unrealistic means of manifesting these images in real life.

You may ask how children can ever hope to experience positive body image when media images and society's messages about beauty are so distorted. Here are a few ways to start:

- Tell your child to act "as if" and to tell herself regularly that she is beautiful even if she feels she's not. Thoughts create reality!
- Tell her not to allow herself any put-downs when she looks in the mirror;
- Don't participate in turning women against each other by comparing their bodies. We all come in different and beautiful shapes and sizes;
- Encourage her to look up to women who are admirable in character, achievements and kindness rather than looks;
- Honestly examine your own feelings as a parent about dieting, weight and body image and get support to change them if they are unhealthy;
- Write to magazines protesting their unrealistic portrayals of the female body;
- If she can't stop repetitive thoughts in her head about feeling fat or ugly, remind her that these thoughts get worse when she is feeling stressed about something unrelated to her body image. Help her talk out what happened that day, or what she is thinking about that is bothersome.

Whatever you do, don't give up. Your child can achieve a healthy body image—it takes constant talking back to negative messages, but she can do it!

Q: How are eating disorders different for boys, and how can we help our son recover quickly?

Statistics show that between 5-10% of anorexics and 4-20% of bulimics are men and boys. Why the large range in percentage? Because boys and men are even more secretive about having an eating disorder than girls and women, and there's no way of knowing how many truly suffer from these illnesses. It's a safe bet to say that the percentages fall in the higher range. Although untrue, males often view eating disorders as "female conditions," adding to the shame they already feel about their eating disordered behaviors. Male populations that are more susceptible to developing eating disorders include athletes, gay males and males in the military (military men have to regularly pass physical readiness tests, and some learn to purge in order to "make weight").

In my practice I find that most teen boys would rather have bamboo shoved under their fingernails than talk about their feelings in counseling. This is why you should choose a therapist that is GOAL ORIENTED with your son, the primary goal being to get out of therapy as soon as he is healthy to do so! Of course, boys still have feelings even if they sometimes don't want to admit it. A skilled therapist will create a delicate balance between not pushing your boy so hard that he resents counseling and refuses to talk, and helping him feel safe and comfortable to seek guidance and support. Don't feel it's inappropriate to ask the potential therapist how she works with boys and if she's sensitive to a boy's different communication style and needs.

It's also important for parents themselves not to mistake eating disorders as a female problem and therefore overlook signs of trouble in their sons. Be especially aware if you have a male athlete, your family has been through a recent trauma (such as death of a loved one, moving, a divorce, or sexual abuse), and/or there have been other family members who have developed eating disorders. In most cases, the signs of an eating disorder and the approaches you should take to helping your son are identical to those that apply to females. The advice in this book is designed to help anyone, son or daughter.

~Five~
Bonus Section

*Seven "Must Read" Tips
For Building Healthy Body Self-Esteem
In Children*

When it comes to healthy eating and positive body image, the good news is that parents have a much greater influence on their kids than they may think. Despite kids' attempts to push against limits and assert their independence, they still look to you for guidance and praise. For that reason it is important that before you consider how you can help your children, you first examine your own behaviors and beliefs about eating and appearance. If you find a lot of negativity and shame in the way you view your own body, get support from a friend or counselor to feel better. You won't be the only person to benefit – your kids will too!

In a culture that is increasingly obsessed with dieting, exercise and the desire to be thin and beautiful, many of us develop our eating habits around the wrong reasons or feel ashamed of our bodies. During the impressionable pre-teen years, kids have an especially heightened risk for acting and feeling this way. It is a time when they desperately want to fit in with their peers, but at the same time feel painfully awkward and self-conscious. In extreme cases, these behaviors and feelings can develop over time into eating disorders.

The good news is that parents can play an essential role in inoculating their children against these serious problems. An eating disorder doesn't just "surface" out of the blue when a child becomes a teenager. It is the result of years of negative messages received from family, peers and the media. Building a child's healthy eating patterns and body self-esteem can start from birth. The pre-teen years are an especially opportune time, since your child is yearning to be independent, but still openly seeks your guidance. Here are some fantastic ways to help your child feel comfortable in her own skin, and to resist the cultural and peer pressure she will likely encounter outside of your home.

1. Build positive and predictable food rituals

In our fast food culture, mealtime in many homes is no longer a time of family togetherness but a chaotic rush before the next activity or a series of lonely meals eaten separately. Try to add a feeling of security to your family and their approach to food by finding your family's own ways to express gratitude for bounty and to appreciate food (after all, we need food in order to live and it's meant to be enjoyed). You can start by giving your child responsibility for one part of each meal, such as saying the blessing, setting the table, or choosing an item for the menu. These simple acts help make mealtime a time when the family accomplishes a common goal and establishes order around the way food is enjoyed.

2. Present foods with variety and an attitude of celebration

Kids innately like to try new things -- all you have to do is put new foods in front of them and they'll usually take a taste. Try to avoid giving in to complaints and providing foods they'll eat with no problems. That may work in the short run, but it could result in unhealthy eating habits which become lifelong. The more variety children enjoy when they're young means they are more likely to enjoy a wide range of foods later on without becoming too finicky. It's better to approach food as a way of enjoying life in its variety, not just as "fuel" to be gobbled down.

3. Avoid labeling certain foods as "forbidden"

Within your value system and dietary restrictions, present all kinds of food in moderation. The key is to set reasonable limits, then let the kids choose freely within them. If, for example, a child is completely restricted from consuming sweets, then the first chance they have to eat them outside of your supervision will likely result in binge eating. In one recent study, two groups of children were brought separately to two rooms filled with goodies (desserts, chips, chocolate, etc.). The first group of children was told to go ahead and take what they desired; the second was ordered to wait 20 minutes before partaking. Which group do you think ended up binge eating? Of course it was the group that was forced to wait. Have faith that when you stock the house with a variety of food choices, your children will learn they will not be deprived, and will subsequently learn to eat in moderation.

3. Do not use food as a reward or a punishment

Although it may be tempting to take away dessert or dinner to punish negative behavior, avoid the impulse. Use other disciplinary tactics, such as removing a favorite activity or TV show for an evening. You want your kids to associate food with sustenance and pleasure, not with sadness, anger, or with pleasing others.

4. Do not pressure your children to lose weight through diet or exercise

Help kids to recognize the feeling of being comfortably satisfied after a meal and to stop eating at that point. As long as they are presented with a variety of foods in moderation, most children will naturally reach and maintain their appropriate body weight. Approach exercise as a fun activity that makes your body feel good, and help children find a type of exercise that doesn't feel like a chore. The real goal of eating and exercise should be, after all, to be healthy and happy, not to look a certain way.

5. Limit the amount of television your child watches

Unfortunately, television and movies are brimming with images of dangerously thin women and muscle-bound men.

When your child does watch TV, help him to challenge these unrealistic and idealized body images. Make an effort to show that people come in all different shapes and sizes, each one valuable and special. Regularly point out positive qualities in others that have nothing to do with physical appearance.

6. Be aware of behaviors and messages you model to your children, both verbal and nonverbal

Try not to give your children negative messages about their eating habits and bodies ("You're eating like a pig;" "You'd be so handsome if you'd just bulk up a little"). Focus more on giving your child positive messages about who he or she is as a person ("You have a beautiful smile," "You are so generous to your friends," "You are a wonderful helper"). Most importantly, try hard not to give your children mixed messages about food and body image. For example, if you tell your daughter she is beautiful, but you are constantly dieting and worrying about your own weight, she will be confused and will have trouble believing what you say about her. Children are far more likely to model their behaviors from what they see their parents do rather than what their parents say.

7. Remember that help is available

Don't feel that you have to handle all problems alone. There are many caring professionals, including pediatricians, therapists and teachers, who possess a wealth of information about these issues. Reaching out to them can often be the best decision you make in supporting your child's personal growth. There are experts who dedicate their careers toward preventing and treating eating disorders, and the amount of guidance you receive from them could mean the difference in the quality of life of your child.

About the Author

Lori Osachy, MSS, LCSW is clinical director of The Body Image Counseling Center of Jacksonville, Florida. A nationally recognized authority in the treatment and prevention of eating disorders, depression, anxiety, and related mental health issues, Lori has successfully counseled adults, children and families for over fifteen years. She regularly lectures and teaches and is the author of numerous articles promoting eating disorders education among health care professionals and the lay population. She has been featured in several national magazines and is a regular mental health consultant for print news and television.

Lori is a graduate of Cornell University and received her Master's degree from Bryn Mawr College Graduate School of Social Work and Social Research. She lives in Jacksonville, Florida where she is a psychotherapist and parent consultant in full-time private practice. Lori's goal is to be able to empower parents and families, providing them with the tools to be successful in overcoming obstacles and to raise happy, healthy kids. Her next project is completing the second book in the Quick Start Recovery series, which is geared towards helping individuals of all ages with eating disorders to quickly begin the process of recovery and experience relief from their symptoms—before they even walk into a therapist's office.